Building Powerful Prayer
for the Younger Gene

Teaching Children to Pray

CHILDREN
ON THE FRONTLINES

CAROL KOCH

Teaching Children to Pray

Published by XP PMinistries
P. O. Box 1017
Maricopa, Arizona 85139
XPministries.com

ISBN: 978-1-621661-56-6

A GENERATIONAL VISION

We are seeing the beginning of an unprecedented global move of God among this current generation of children. Joel prophesied this when he wrote, "And it shall come to pass in the last days, says God, that I will pour out My Spirit on all flesh; your sons and daughters shall prophesy, your old men shall dream dreams, your young men shall see visions" (Joel 2:28). Our children have been called to walk in the things of God. We have the privilege to equip them with the foundational principles of the Word of God.

If you do not think our children are facing spiritual battles, please re-read your newspaper! Daily, our children face a culture that no one could even dream of 50 years ago: guns in schools, drugs, cutting, and super-sexualized messages that de-rail lives coming from all forms of media. It makes you wonder just how important this generation must be for so many weapons to be formed against it! If our children are to handle life in modern society and to walk in the good works which God has already ordained for them to do, (Ephesians 2:10) the church must make room for them to **realize their full spiritual potential. It requires a new way of thinking and of viewing our children. They're not just small people who need to be entertained while the adults learn spiritual truths. Each child is an important part of the church body, with a God-given destiny that begins in childhood. They need to learn all they can about the ways of God as soon as they can; their very lives, and the life of the church depend upon it.**

So our vision for this manual encompasses far more than just starting a nice little prayer group for the kids in your church. Our hope is that you will use it as a tool to build, build, build a structure that will house a children's prayer movement in your region. We long to help you equip a generation who will turn to the Lord with all their heart, with all their soul, and with all their might. We want children with tender hearts who will seek after His presence, have a desire to do what is right in the eyes of the Lord, walk in His ways, and will not turn to the right or to the left.

Oh, that the children would taste
and see that He is good!

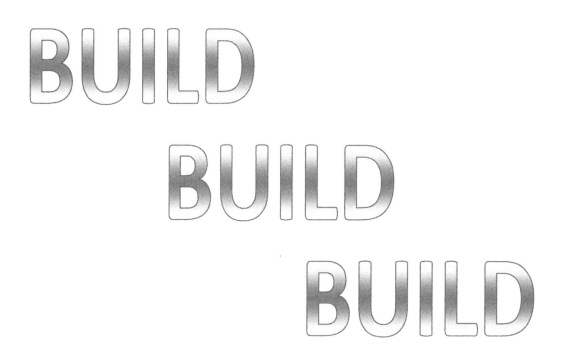

TABLE OF CONTENTS

INTRODUCTION

"I Will Do It, But Only Until Easter"

I will never forget one particular night. I was in our church auditorium during our midweek service. We were 15 minutes into the service when I saw the midweek children's leader rushing through the back, with a fast-food sack in hand, dragging her children behind her, hoping to come up with something to fill the time requirement for the evening.

At the time, I sensed there was something wrong with this picture, but I thought, "Oh well, at least someone is taking the kids." As senior pastors of a suburban, middle-class congregation, my husband and I had our share of challenges. As is typical in many churches, we were often short of children's workers for the midweek service. Not too long after this incident, that children's leader resigned her position saying she just couldn't do it anymore. My first thought was, "Here we go again. The children's area has been dumped **again**!"

We have always believed in the validity of children's ministry and have strived to support the children's workers in any way we could. So we immediately began the big hunt to find **someone** to fill the void. We tried every form of recruitment known to senior pastors – guilt, pressure, nagging, and even begging; however, none of these tactics seemed to work this time.

During this time, my 10 year-old daughter had a dream. In the dream, our church kids were in a room in the educational wing. Two men with guns came into the room and started shooting at the children. In the dream, the men were unable to kill them physically. I knew immediately the dream was from the Lord and I discerned He was showing us that the enemy was trying to spiritually take out (kill) that age group. Something rose up inside of me, a tenacity – I was **not** going to allow the enemy to succeed!

I ended up making a statement, which at the time, I had no idea would become part of my destiny. I blurted out, **"I will do it. I'll take on the children, but only until Easter."** (Easter was just a few months away and I thought surely by then we would find someone else).

The Lord held me accountable to my statement, which then led to a serious debate (complaining) with Him. "But God, I'm not trained for children's ministry. I'm not very good." I continued, "God, I don't even like to work with the children. I'm not even fun. So what am I supposed to do?" And then, closest to an audible voice of God I had ever heard, HE spoke to me! The word I heard was, "SHHHHH!!!" In other words, "Be quiet and listen." He said gently, but extremely powerfully, "Just pour into them what's in you." Instantly, all anxiety and doubt disappeared, "Oh! I can do that!" I responded. From that moment on, it was like, " I got it!" I stopped my complaining! God had given me my mandate and I was going to carry it out to the best of my ability and with the resources I had at the time.

And so it began! At that time we met on the typical Wednesday evening church night. The children and I would experience God in whichever way I had experienced Him earlier in the week. No one had ever told me that kids couldn't or shouldn't experience God. When He taught me about worship, I taught them about worship. When He emphasized the Father's heart to me, I emphasized it to them. My focus became "Oh that these children would taste and see that the Lord is good." I knew that if they could just experience His presence, their hearts would be forever turned toward Him.

The children readily received everything the Lord had in store for us. Much to my surprise, the children began worshipping wholeheartedly. They began to hear Him speaking to them individually. They began to move in the things of the Spirit, such as prophesying, seeing visions, praying for the sick, and even evangelizing. Week after week they continued to have personal encounters and experiences with the Lord. An awakening in the hearts of the children had occurred.

I knew if they could just experience His presence, their hearts would be forever turned toward Him.

To our great delight, this awakening spilled over into our Sunday morning services. Instead of the children fidgeting restlessly until the worship was over, they quickly and willingly entered into and participated in all aspects of the service. It is their service just as much as it is the adult's service. As a result, our entire church body has been greatly impacted, becoming champions for the next generation.

Of course, there is much more to this journey than I have just mentioned. In this school, we will cover a lot of the foundational building blocks that brought us to this place.

You see, I believe we are getting ready to witness one of the greatest children's movements we have ever seen. Never in the history of the world has there been such an emphasis on children as there is now. This movement is so real to me, I feel like my call is to be a "Voice for the children in the body of Christ!"

So get ready! This manual contains both foundational building blocks and a key for the children in our land to be a part of spiritual history. Change the world we live in by using these foundational building blocks to build, build, build a structure that will house a mighty move of God through the children. Take this key and use it to unlock an awakening in an entire generation and change the course of history forever!

"Equipping children...
You're going to equip the next generation...
You're going to equip the small children into the apostolic, into the prophetic, into the move of healing..."

- PROPHETIC WORD GIVEN BY CAL PIERCE TO PASTORS ALAN AND CAROL

CHAPTER 1

A SPARK STARTS THE FLAME

Our children's prayer group officially began in June of 2002. However, the groundwork and foundations were put into place several years earlier when we began pouring into the children on a regular basis, teaching them about the things of the Spirit and giving them weekly opportunities to worship on **their** level. We built relationships with them, encouraged them in their spiritual walks, and taught them the Word.

In June of 2002, we invited international children's minister Becky Fischer of Kids In Ministry International to conduct a Kid's Conference at our church. What happened next took us all by surprise; it wasn't a little Bible story, with crafts, games and snacks, (which I'm not opposed to having). Rather, it was children worshipping with their whole hearts, Bible teaching, and ministry with depth and presented in a way they could relate to. The children were so touched by God that the conference brought our whole group up a level in their relationship with God. One evening, several children were praying and weeping over the nations. At the conclusion, we were determined to not let this level of spiritual intensity die off. It was like the kids were "catapulted" into a deeper level. We wanted to do even more than just maintain this; we wanted to go further. To accomplish this, I knew something had to be added. After praying I felt like the answer was prayer - a separate kid's prayer group.

We began simply, using the learning center concept (which we refer to as **Prayer Stations**) and as the weeks and months progressed, we were able to advance deeper and deeper into the things of the Lord with the children. It became easier and easier to lead them **in** worship, intercession, and His presence.

We now have a core group of children who meet weekly to spend time with the Lord seeking His face and His heart to see what He would have them pray. Some weeks, the entire group will lie quietly before the Lord for almost 90 minutes, listening to Him and enjoying His presence. Other weeks, there will be worship and intense prayer over a specific area or prayer over the nations and current events (elections, selecting of the pope, natural disasters).

Even more importantly, we are helping to captivate their hearts to the Lord. We are giving these children all the tools and practice they need to be champions in the Kingdom of God. We are not only teaching them to pray, we are training them to use their gifts in intercession and equipping them with the tools they need for a life-long adventure with the Lord. They are **"tasting and seeing that the Lord is good"** and are forever turning their hearts toward Him.

It is our desire that this manual will equip you to begin your own adventure with your kids in the area of intercession. Although there have been a few "bumps" along the road, the rewards and benefits we have seen in our children far outweigh any obstacles we faced. We have tried to include as many practical tips as feasible and as much vision and insight as possible to enable you to quickly become an effective equipper of your own and to begin reaping the rewards of starting your own children's prayer group.

CHAPTER 2

WHY PRAYER?

Prayer has always been an important part of my life, a passion of mine. There are probably two main reasons for that. One reason was my older sister who took it upon herself to pour into me and make me hungry for prayer. Simply put, mentoring, which is what this manual is all about.

Another reason was a teaching on prayer titled, *Could You Not Tarry One Hour?* authored by Dr. Larry Lea, which was popular in the 1980s. The teaching, which included the importance and understanding of an effectual prayer life, created in me a desire to be a person of prayer.

SO BACK TO THE QUESTION, WHY PRAYER?

1. Prayer develops a personal relationship with God. They talk to Him, He talks to them. That is how any friendship is developed – through dialogue.

2. When relationship is established, the giftings and callings are the outgrowth of relationship – not based on performance or learned behavior.

3. Prayer is a "springboard" into the spiritual gifts. The gifts naturally happen when focusing on Jesus instead of seeking just gifts.

4. Prayer is a tool for developing a "hearing ear." It teaches you to learn to listen, not just do all the talking.

5. Prayer is something that can be done anytime, anywhere, under any circumstance. It can be done out loud or quietly.

 6. A developed prayer life will "capture" their heart. It will take head knowledge and transfer it to the heart. They will "taste and see" that God is good! (Psalms 34:8.) I think it is so important that children know and experience that God loves them just because they are them and not based on how good their works are.

God so put it on my heart to teach a generation of children how to pray. I thought, "How is that supposed to happen? Sounds awesome, but how?"

During that time I was leading a ladies' prayer group. That particular day, I asked the group if we could go into the children's area and pray for some insight to the prayer piece. As we were interceding, I received a "download" on how to practically teach small children prayer.

I was reminded of my oldest daughter when she was four years old. She attended a Christian preschool. One day I went to observe her; I just wanted to spend time to see what she was learning. The preschool was set up with learning centers where they would move from center to center, topic to topic, and have hands-on activities to learn a particular skill. God showed me that if it works for learning basic, intelligible truths, then why couldn't the same concept work for spiritual truths? In other words, why re-invent the wheel? The kid's prayer was born using the learning center concept, which we refer to as **prayer stations**. And it works very well, I might add.

In some ways, it's like when the disciples asked Jesus to teach them to pray. He gave them a pattern they could relate to. It taught them the basic foundations of establishing a prayer life. The prayer stations are the same concept; it's a learning style they can learn from as a child.

Whatever you pray for, you also develop a heart for. Whatever area it is, include a Scripture that backs up why you believe the things you are praying for. For example, at the healing station, why do you pray for healing? In Isaiah 53:5, it says, "by His stripes we are healed." You are building a foundational belief structure based on the Word of God. Plus, they are learning the Bible in a fun way.

NURSERY - CHARACTER

Before explaining about the prayer centers, I want to "back the truck up", so to speak. To be the most effective, it's important to start at the beginning.

We begin pouring into our children while they are still babies in the nursery. We believe their spirits are able to receive and respond even before they are able to talk. Many churches view the nursery and preschool program as a ministry to the *parents*. We believe it is a ministry *to the children* and treat it accordingly by caring for their spiritual needs as well as their physical needs.

When the children are two and three years old, we teach a basic program every week with the "See and Know" curriculum. This curriculum uses pictures on poster board and simple songs to teach the toddlers foundational truths. Every week they are taught one of the following: Story of Creation, God Made You, God Loves You, The Bible Is God's Word, God Gives You Good Things, God Sent Jesus as a Baby, Jesus Grew into a Man, Jesus Died for You, Jesus Is Building a House for You, and The Holy Spirit Lives Inside of You, God Knows, God Cares. The children absolutely love this program! The pictures are simple yet colorful. The songs are easy to remember. The truths are going deep into their minds and spirits at this very early age. Singing the same songs over and over enables them to confess foundational truths while they are very young. The Word is being poured into them and godly character traits are being built in them.

They still have color sheets, crafts, snacks, and playtime because we recognize the nature of toddlers. At the same time, we have had powerful times when the presence of the Lord was very strong. One Sunday morning, the toddlers began praying for sick children. The teacher recognized a heavy healing anointing present on the children and notified the adult service. A significant number of adults went to the nursery to receive prayer *by the toddlers* and many were healed!

PRESCHOOL - CHARACTER

Our 4 & 5 year olds are taught Bible stories, character traits, and beginning principles concerning living a Christian life. This is the class where we see the most salvations occur. Many of the children have been brought up in church since birth, and when they reach this age, they realize their need for a Savior. We lead them in a simple prayer of salvation and then treat them as we would treat any new convert: by teaching them basic Bible disciplines. They are taught to pray, to read their Bibles (even if it is a picture Bible), to give, to serve, to worship, to witness. We teach them to share, to forgive, and to be a blessing to their family. We continue building godly character and train them to walk in love.

These children are very serious about their faith. They are eager to learn and even more eager to put what they learn into practice. They love to pray for each other and anyone else who has a need. They are completely open to the Lord and accept His Word unconditionally. They often see in the spirit realm. One little boy told about "the man with the glowing face" who was with him at the airport and theme park during his family's vacation. (The child's mother had specifically prayed angelic protection around him during their vacation and the child was seeing the results of her prayers.)

The Nursery and Preschool leg is so important because it is the foundation, the cornerstone of what we are trying to build. These children are like little buckets, waiting to be filled. We fill the entire "bucket" – body, soul, and spirit. We begin using the Word to build godly character in them. We let them taste and see that the Lord is good because He *is* good – especially including those under the age of six!

SUNDAY MORNINGS – THE WORD

On Sunday mornings, our elementary age children participate in the worship portion of the service with the teenagers and adults. At the conclusion of worship, Kindergarten through fourth graders are dismissed for Children's Church and fifth and sixth graders are dismissed for a more traditional Sunday School type class. Both of these classes focus on the Word. We don't just teach Bible stories but also principles of the Word. We teach them to hear God's voice, to read and study their Bibles, to worship God. We give them monthly Bible reading schedules and reward those who complete it with a prize.

We carefully consider *how* we teach each week. For instance, when we teach on forgiveness, we do not spend the entire service telling them they should forgive each other. Instead, *we teach them how to forgive*: what to say, how to resist the enemy, how to walk in forgiveness, and more. And we back it all up with the Word. When we teach on faith, we teach them how to increase their faith - praying in tongues, speaking words of life, reading the Word. Of course all of this teaching is done using kid-friendly methods such as puppet skits, drama skits, object lessons, games and contests; whatever methods are relevant at the time. Our primary focus is not to entertain the children, but to instill in them a life-long love relationship with the Lord and His Word!

Our focus for the Sunday morning classes is so crucial because it ensures that our children are grounded and balanced in the Word. As they move out in the things of the Spirit, they can measure their experiences with the standard of the Word. It is a tool to help them discern whether things are of the Lord or not, and is a protection to help keep their motives pure. Without this continual teaching of the Word, we would not be able to progress in the area of prayer with much success. The children could quickly become off-balance which would not be pleasing to the Lord. Since we do spend so much time in the Word, these children are having firm supports being built into them. These supports give them stability and strength and allow them to go further and deeper in the things of the Lord.

> *"Thy Word is a lamp to my feet and a light to my path..."*
> — PSALMS 119:105

MID-WEEK PRAYER

The children learn ALL AREAS OF PRAYER DURING THIS TRAINING TIME. They have their own worship service apart from the adults. The focus isn't worship, but it's important to help create an atmosphere for prayer. It also helps to get their attention to focus on God and what He's saying. *(More on the topic of worship later on in this manual.)*

This group is very similar to a cell group or home group. It is held in the same room as children's church, so they are familiar with the room. It is comfortable to them, so they feel safe to try new and different things. We encourage them to worship the Lord with all their heart, soul, mind, and body. This is the true spiritual training ground. This is where they learn to express themselves in worship, to listen to God's voice, to respond to Him, to worship and praise Him. They learn to become comfortable operating in the gifts of the Spirit so that it becomes very natural to them. Reluctance, self-consciousness, and shyness are replaced with boldness and self-confidence. It then becomes very easy for them to transition to participating in the Sunday morning worship service with the adults.

On prayer evenings, we teach on various topics of prayer as the Lord leads us. It is so important for the children to be trained in every area of prayer. We have done it all, from praying for the sick, to prayer walking, praying in front of our city hall, taking a bus to our state capital praying on the steps of it. We have organized a trip to Washington D.C. to develop a heart for our country and to pray for it.

This mentoring time is crucial because it allows the children to practice. It allows them the freedom to explore, to try new things, to even fail, all in a safe place. They are seldom embarrassed or even self-conscious. It is very easy for them to participate. I want them to know that Jesus is the Light and He lives in them. That is their confidence!

I refer to building this in your church but what I like about this topic is that it is NOT just for the local church setting. I believe churches should offer prayer training for children. But this can be done anywhere. Just take the same principles and use it in home school, in missions, cell groups, home churches, and the list is endless! Even at home with your own children or grandchildren.

BUILDING YOUR STRUCTURE

You may already have a structure in place at your church. If so, you are ready to go start a dynamic prayer group and can expect amazing results! If you do not have a children's prayer group in your church, we encourage you to prayerfully consider working to build this foundation. Work within the existing programs to teach your children the Word and how to operate in the gifts of the Spirit. Instil in them a love for the Word, a desire to please the Lord, and a willingness to obey Him. Build the foundation and the supports before you put the roof on the house!

CHAPTER 3

PRAYER STATIONS

OUR GOAL

When we started our prayer group, we did not want to spend a lot of time teaching or lecturing our children about prayer. They knew the necessity and validity of prayer (as mentioned earlier, the foundation had already been laid). We did not need them to learn **about** prayer – we wanted them to learn **to pray.** We wanted to bring the principles of prayer into their world and make it relevant for them.

We also wanted to build in our children a heart for the things we believed were important to God and on His heart. We wanted them to build their own personal relationship and know from the Word why they believed the things they did. Prayer will help to establish that.

I'll never forget one particular time - I was in Canada teaching this manual and had some sessions with the kids. I had a teaching with the kids on listening (soaking) prayer; it's such a wonderful tool on helping them hear the still small voice of God. After it was over, I asked (as I always do) if they had heard anything. One little girl around 4 or 5 years old raised her hand, with tears in her eyes, and said, "I heard God tell me He loved me for the very first time." WOW!! Can you image how that changed her life, experiencing that at such an early age? I have many testimonies of the fruit of equipping children in the area of prayer.

WHAT IS A PRAYER STATION?

As we sought the Lord for direction concerning this prayer group, He led us to the pattern of **learning centers**. A learning center is a table or small area supplied with a variety of materials and activities built around a common theme. A typical learning center classroom is composed of several of these centers. The students visit each learning center for a period of time, focusing on the particular center's theme. This concept is a very effective tool used in many learning environments and is easy to implement.

In our prayer group, we refer to our learning centers as **Prayer Stations**. We supplied each Prayer Station with various objects and pictures to give the children a point of contact for their prayers. We don't use the objects and pictures to play with or to entertain. Their purpose is to stimulate the children's minds and bodies and help them to focus on praying for one area at a time. For example, when praying for the President of the United States, they hold a picture of him in their hands. We have found it to be extremely effective in encouraging the children to pray and in helping them to maintain their focus.

HOW WE USE THEM

When we use the prayer stations, we usually start our prayer group with everyone together with worship music playing softly in the background. At this time we give a small amount of instruction. Then we remind them this is not playtime and it is God's time. Sometimes we direct the children to go somewhere in the room and spend a few minutes quieting their bodies and minds before the Lord. Then we gather back together as a group and begin praying. We invite Holy Spirit to come and lead and direct us and ask Him to help us focus in on Him.

During the first several weeks, we would go as a group from station to station, spending ten minutes or so at each one. We focused on one area for a short period of time and then moved on to the next station. Moving from station to station allows the kids to move around and also provides them practice in learning to tune in to the Lord.

We invite Holy Spirit to come and lead and direct us and ask Him to help us focus in on Him.

After we have prayed at all of the stations, we spend time praying for each other using the topic we are focusing on. For example, if we are at the healing center we see if anyone needs prayer for sickness or for a family member. It's important to do things differently sometimes, just to mix it up. It keeps it fun.

A few minutes before quitting, we pull the kids back together and ask them if the Lord has spoken to them or shown them anything they want to share. We are often amazed at the depth of things the Lord has shown and spoken to them. We write down anything the Holy Spirit seemed to emphasize - often there has been a recurring theme. Interestingly, the Lord will often emphasize that theme during the following Sunday morning service.

We usually close with a simple prayer of thanks. Afterwards, the children help put away the various Prayer Station items and supplies. On special occasions, we serve snacks. Once they developed a heart for prayer, snacks became very unimportant to them. Remember, this is a pattern to establish the foundational principal of prayer. As you learn the pattern, ask the Lord for creativity and expand the basic model.

CHOOSING THEMES

When we created our Prayer Stations, we first thought about what was important to our church and which characteristics set us apart from other local bodies. Christ Triumphant Church has always had a heart for Lee's Summit and we want to be an agent of revival for our city and the surrounding area. Our church also has a heart for the nations demonstrated by supporting numerous missionaries and organizations in our own country and foreign countries. And finally, we have a strong emphasis on healing. Throughout the years, we have received many prophetic words referring to our church as a Healing Station.

With these distinguishing characteristics in mind, we created the following Prayer Stations:

- ❖ NATIONS
- ❖ HEALING
- ❖ SOUL TREE
- ❖ CITY
- ❖ CHURCH FAMILY

PRAYING FOR THE NATIONS

We gathered a globe, a map of the United States, several small flags from various nations including Israel, a picture of the current president, a pad of sticky-notes in the shape of the world, pencils, and several Bibles.

We instruct the children to ask the Lord to give them a country to pray for and to write their name and country on one of the sticky-notes and put it in the basket. Each week we pull out those notes and pray over those countries. Sometimes we ask the Lord to give us verses for those countries, which we write down on the sticky-notes. We also lay hands on the countries on the globe and pray in the Spirit over them. Sometimes we speak the Word over the countries.

We encourage the children to pray for godly leadership and for souls to be saved. We bless Israel and pray for peace in her streets. We pray for protection for our president, for wise counsel and godly decisions. We encourage the children to research the country God puts on their heart.

HEALING STATION

We put a First Aid kit, a box of Band-Aids, a small bottle of anointing oil, and paper towels at this station. In the beginning we instructed the

kids to anoint a Band-Aid with oil and to pray for someone they knew who needed healing. They loved doing this and we began using pieces of cloth and anointing them as well. We taught them that this took place in the Bible in Acts 19:11-12, that people were healed

and now they have seen people healed as well!

Sometimes we focus together on someone in our church family, and other times we just let them pray individually. We quickly learned it was not necessary for them to give us all the details, we just have them pray for the person and the rest of the group agrees. At first, we would tell the children what the Bible says about healing, using different verses each week. After several weeks, we started asking, "*What does the Bible say about healing?*" or "*Why are we praying for healing?*" and then they would respond with the Word.

SOUL TREE STATION

We created a **Soul Tree** by using a bare tree branch stuck in a plastic bucket with plaster of Paris (found in a church closet). We took the tree and several pairs of old tennis shoes and a permanent marker and put them in this station. We told the kids to write on the sole of the shoe the name of someone who needed to ask Jesus in their hearts. We then used the shoes as points of contact to pray for the salvation of those souls. When the person gets saved, we write their name on apple-shaped paper, hang it on the tree, and throw the shoe away. It's a tangible way for the kids to monitor their prayer requests and answers. Once again, we use different verses to pray – "*Open the eyes of their heart Lord*" or "*Lord, transfer them from the dominion of darkness to the kingdom of light.*" Just be sensitive to the voice of the Holy Spirit - it's amazing what He will show the kids to pray.

OUR CITY STATION

For this station, we marked our church's location on a street map of Lee's Summit and laid the map on the floor. A key prophetic word dealt with our city being a place of much angelic activity so we set two angel Christmas tree ornaments on the corners of the map. This teaches them to learn to pray according to prophetic promises (I Timothy 1:18)! We also included flashlights and a set of plastic ears. We instruct the children to shine the flashlight

on various portions of the map and to ask God to "*shine Your light on Lee's Summit.*" We let them put ears on and pray that "*Lee's Summit would have ears to hear Your voice, Lord.*" We pray for the government, schools, and for other churches. We ask for angelic protection and angelic visitation and we pray for revival in Lee's Summit.

> "*Seek the peace and prosperity of the city which I have sent you to. Pray to the Lord for it...*"
>
> **- JEREMIAH 29:7**

CHURCH FAMILY STATION

This station simply contains a church pictorial directory, a candle, and bricks with the words "LOVE" and "UNITY" on them. We teach the kids to pray for our church leadership – the pastors, elders, ministry heads and their families. We encourage them to bless our church and all who are under its "umbrella." We pray that everything in our church would be built on love and done in unity. We pray for increase and that we would always please Him.

Whenever we have outreaches or specific needs in the church, we pray for those as well – even if the outreach or event does not include or involve the children. They especially love praying for the youth functions and outreaches. We do this to develop a heart for all areas of our church.

YOUR PRAYER STATIONS

We encourage you to seek the Lord about the theme and content of your Prayer Stations. Think about the foundational areas of your church. Consider which areas you want to emphasize, and build a station around them so your children will develop a heart for them. You will be amazed at how interested your children will become in the life of your church once they start praying for these areas. Not only will they want to pray for them, they also will want to participate in the areas!

In order for the Prayer Stations to be effective, they need to be relevant to your children. In order to make them relevant, you will need to personalize them. In other words, the station should connect the children to the prayer focus. Whenever possible, photographs of the people you are praying for should be included in the station. Give your children information to peak their curiosity, stir their compassion, or open their eyes to injustice (hunger, poverty, lack of religious freedom, lack of believers). They especially like to hear stories and information about other children. All of this is done to motivate them to pray sincerely for these areas.

Consider the areas foundational to your church or ministry – what was the vision for your church when it was started? Try to incorporate these areas into a prayer station. Perhaps your church has a heart for ministry to the poor, the homeless, or the elderly. Create a prayer station for one of these ministries. Does your church have a relationship with a specific missionary or organization? Or do you have former church members who are now missionaries? Use photographs, pictures, maps, and items to represent their ministry or country. Choose Israel or any country you personally have a connection with if your church does not have any other missionary connections.

You can be very creative with your Prayer Stations but they don't have to be elaborate or expensive. We spent very little money by using items we already owned. If you lack specific items, enlist the help of your congregation. Many of our church members have given us souvenirs, flags, and banners from foreign countries. Keep the Prayer Stations simple so they are easy to set up and take down. Don't get sidetracked into an entertaining mode; remember the purpose of having items is to give your children a point of contact for their prayers.

If your children are not familiar with the Bible verses, print out a list of the pertinent ones. You can also write the verses out on 3"x5" cards to include with the various stations. The children can then read/pray the verses aloud until they learn them well enough to pray them by memory.

You can also find a lot of material on the Internet. Pictures, maps, and current event information are very easy to obtain. The Presidential Prayer Network will send you a weekly e-mail with specific areas to pray for the United States government and you can incorporate these into your group's prayers.

There are several websites with schedules and suggested areas to pray for foreign countries. Try to keep current and be relevant.

CHAPTER 4

HOW TO BEGIN

You can start a children's prayer group with very little money or manpower. There are several keys to making a successful children's prayer group.

WHAT DO I NEED TO GET STARTED?

1. A qualified leader. We believe the leader should possess the following characteristics:

   - *The leader needs to be someone who is an intercessor or has a heart for intercession. Without a heart for intercession, you can't impart something you don't have.*
   - *The leader needs to be able to commit to the group on a weekly basis for at least a year. This commitment will allow the children to develop a close relationship with the leader.*
   - *The leader should have some experience working with children or have a heart for children. This group is not really the place for someone who is inexperienced with children. The leader needs to understand how they function and behave, and needs to be able to relate well to them.*
   - *The leader needs to be able to flow in the Spirit in a balanced way, completely grounded in the Word.*
   - *The leader needs to be flexible – able to follow Holy Spirit's leading and not set on accomplishing their agenda.*

In other words, the leader needs to be someone you want the children to imitate, because that is exactly what will happen.

2. A place or room to meet in every week. It should be large enough to accommodate your group but small enough to provide an intimate atmosphere. Meeting on the same day and time in the same room will provide stability and familiarity for your group.

3. Some form of worship music. Determine whether pre-recorded music or a live worship team will be used. If you choose live music, make sure they pick music relevant to that age group.

4. A few basic supplies such as:
   - Bibles
   - Paper, pens, or pencils
   - Markers
   - Praise instruments, flags, or banners
   - Objects for your Prayer Stations
   - Notebook for recording insights, visions, pictures, etc.

5. Additional supplies can be added as needed:
   - Hand-held tape/digital recorder (to record significant words or times of intense prayer), cell phones, etc.
   - Maps and/or a globe
   - Some form of keeping track of answered prayers
   - Additional praise instruments or armor
   - Pillows or beanbag chairs

STEPS TO BEGIN A GROUP

1. You must have the blessing and permission from your church leadership. Please read the chapter in this manual concerning working within the framework of your church government.

2. Decide on your Prayer Stations. Gather your supplies.

3. Select a leader, secure your room, choose a date and time.

4. Promote your group! In an excited manner, tell the kids at your church about your prayer group. Give them vision for what will take place. Share testimonies as the kids have experiences to share.

5. Specifically invite children you think or sense are intercessors. Talk to their parents and ask them to bring their children. If your church is large and you think you might have too big of a response, then start with a manageable number by inviting only a few children. You can always open it up to the entire group later or start another group. Do not feel obligated to include all of the children in your church. Not everyone will be at the proper spiritual maturity level and not everyone will have an interest in praying for an hour or more. That's okay! On the other hand, if you have only two or three children, that's okay too! Start small and build a core group. Trust the Lord to bring the increase and concentrate on the ones He's given to you now!

6. Prepare. Most of what you will do with this prayer group will come from the overflow of your personal walk with the Lord. Ask Him to show you what is on His heart for this prayer group this week. Spend time in His presence and in His Word so that you are tuned in to His

Holy Spirit. Pray in tongues. Keep your spiritual "antennas" up. See what God is doing and use it with your kids.

6. Consider asking "seasoned" prayer warriors in your church to commit to pray for this area and <u>with</u> them. Keep them informed on what God is doing. This is a way for the <u>whole</u> church to be involved and another way to link the generations together.

KID'S CONFERENCE ON ISRAEL

YOUR FIRST MEETING

1. The leader should arrive early and get the room completely set up before any of the children arrive. Put any potentially distracting items away. Get the worship music cued up or discuss with your worship team your anticipated plan. Make sure the sound system is working and check the temperature of the room.

2. Greet each child enthusiastically as they arrive. Give special attention to anyone appearing reluctant. Suggest that all get a drink and use the restroom before the meeting gets started. Make it fun!

3. It is important to start off right. Lay the groundwork with a few rules (given in a gentle manner) and expected behavior. Give a little instruction with a lot of encouragement, *"We're going to have a great time with the Lord,"* *"God is going to move powerfully tonight"* or *"I'm so excited about this prayer group!"* Introduce the various Prayer Stations and explain their purpose and how to use the objects at each station. (You might also need to explain how they are NOT going to use them - i.e. *"Do not shine the flashlight into each other's eyes",* or *"Do not hit anyone with the swords."* Remember that they are still children!)

4. Follow the pattern we used with worship and the Prayer Stations or create your own pattern. Knowing how long to stay at each prayer station is a skill the leader will have to develop. You want to stay long enough to accomplish what the Lord intended, but not so long that you lose everyone's interest. Some of your children will lose interest fairly quickly, and some will be able to stay at one station the entire time without losing focus. Concentrate on the group of children who do not fall into either category. You need to shift to another station when those children begin to lose interest. If you believe the Lord has more to

accomplish, then pull the disengaged ones back in, *"You know what? I don't think the Lord is done yet with this Prayer Station. Let's all come back here and ask if there is another verse or something else He wants you to pray."*

5. Start and end on time. The Lord is aware of your time constraints and is completely able to move powerfully within them! Even spiritually mature children still have limited attention spans. You don't want to wait until everyone is bored or exhausted before ending. You need to end on a positive note with them wanting to come back for more!

6. Try to spend a few minutes, towards the end, allowing the children to share what the Lord showed them. You might want to journal these insights.

7. Before you dismiss the children, be sure to encourage and exhort them and praise them for working so hard.

8. Serving snacks is something you can do. Sometimes I give them a snack at the end. Whatever works best for your group.

After your first prayer meeting is over, take a little time to review and evaluate. What worked? What didn't? Do you need to change, add, or delete any of the objects in your Prayer Stations? Did the worship music enhance or distract? How many of the children participated? What was their level of participation? Ask the Lord to show you what, if anything, needs to be changed.

CHAPTER 5

WORSHIP

Appropriate worship music is crucial to the effectiveness of your prayer group. Worship music will help to set the tone of your meeting and usher in the presence of the Lord. It will enable you to bring everyone together and focus on the Lord together.

Begin with using the resources that you have at your disposal right now. If you do not have musicians and a worship team, start with using CDs or DVDs. Pick something with "the breath of God" on them. If the Lord is leading you into a quiet time, then choose calm, soothing music. If the Lord is leading your group into spiritual warfare, then choose music with a strong beat. As Holy Spirit directs the prayer, you can easily/quickly change the type of song. Eventually, when you can, develop a worship team that incorporates some of the children as well. These are your future leaders!

SELECTING WORSHIP MUSIC

1. Select songs familiar to your children – ones you sing in church or other current songs they are familiar with or listen to on the radio.

2. Pick anointed songs that touch the children's heart when they hear them.

3. Choose songs that are easy to sing with catchy choruses.

4. We do not use many traditional children's songs, as they often do not encourage an attitude of worship. I have a youth pick out songs that are current and that the age group can relate to.

5. Be prepared to explain difficult words or symbolic phrases. For example, the phrase, "Let it rain" refers to the Lord's presence and not the weather!

6. Create simple actions to accompany the songs. Group actions will help the children become less self-conscious about moving their bodies in worship. It gets them used to movement in worship and helps them to participate.

WORSHIP TEAMS

If you decide to use a live worship team, select your members carefully. Choose someone who can lead others in worship, flows in the Spirit, and believes in the value of children praying. Your worship team will also need to be flexible and have a wide repertoire of music (fast, slow, warfare, majesty, intimate). Work with them on the selection of music and songs, giving them specific instructions.

You may have a talented older child or teen in your congregation who would love to help you lead worship. If this child/teen will follow your lead and submit to your instruction, then go for it! Not only will you be equipping your children to pray, you will also be equipping this young person as a worship leader! I love having the youth as my leaders.

FLAGS, BANNERS, AND MORE

Another worship component can be the use of flags, banners, and praise instruments. There is an assortment of simple, child-sized flags and banners made out of solid-colored fabric and dowel rods. You can use them during worship and intercession in several different ways. Sometimes they are just used to wave in the air, to celebrate the Lord. At other times, specific flags are used for specific reasons in intercession.

We also use sets of plastic armor and plastic swords. The boys really enjoy using these "weapons." They like to march around the room, swinging and lunging with the swords. One song, "The Sound of a Warrior," has been especially effective in engaging the boys. We have had powerful times of intercession as the boys swing the swords and "cut off" the enemy and his schemes.

We usually remind them of the seriousness of their actions, *"Remember! We're not just playing! We're attacking the enemy and all of his plans!"* At times we have encouraged them to call out the "enemies" they are slaying. One week we were praying for an upcoming healing conference and these boys started shouting out sicknesses such as asthma, diabetes, cancer, muscular dystrophy, blindness, and ALS. We had expected to hear "minor" illnesses such as colds and allergies, but they were going after the giants!

ADDITIONAL WORSHIP RESOURCES

There are many sources available to help you find appropriate and meaningful worship music. The worship leader at your church might have resources you could use. Most Christian bookstores will allow you to listen to the CDs before purchasing them and there are several worship music web-sites available on the internet. Download songs on your phone; you can take that in any area.

Worship is a vital part of the prayer group meeting. Look for ways to encourage your children to worship but don't feel as if you have to have everything in place before beginning your prayer group. Your goal for worship is to enhance the intercession and not to distract or take away from the intercession. Start with what you have and gradually add to your collection. **Start simple and build!**

CHAPTER 6

CORRECTING WITHOUT CRUSHING

Perhaps the biggest challenge in equipping a group of children to pray is how to properly maintain balance. You want to encourage them to be bold and move in the things of the Spirit freely. You want them to be spiritually mature, yet at the same time, you have to recognize they are still physically and emotionally immature. You want them to be all that they can be without putting pressure on them or having too high of an expectation.

As a leader, maintaining this balance can sometimes seem overwhelming. We have found a way to maintain this balance, which we like to call "spiritual mothering and fathering." We watch over the children and try to draw out all God has for them. We recognize both their future destinies and their current limitations. We are firm, but never harsh. We have expectations for their attitudes and behavior but are never unrealistic or legalistic. We affirm and encourage and gently steer them in the right direction when we sense someone is veering off course. We nurture, guide, and equip them all at the same time.

> *We watch over the children and try to draw out all God has for them.*

We want the children to always feel free to express themselves and to speak what they believe God is saying to them. We also make sure what they say and do always line up with the Word and is done with the right heart attitude. ***The key is to instruct, encourage, and correct in such a way that will not stifle the Holy Spirit or crush their spirits.***

GUIDELINES TO MAINTAINING BALANCE

1. **Consistency is the key!** There must be one adult leader there week after week after week. This is absolutely vital to the success of your group! The leader must develop a close relationship with the children and build a high level of trust with them. Children will not share things of the Spirit or receive correction well from adults they do not know and trust. It will take a long time to develop relationships and build trust if there is a different leader every week. Children need consistency. Multiple leaders will each operate differently, even if they are following the same schedule and format. There is a time and place for variety, but it is not by having several leaders.

   Another benefit to having consistent leadership is that you will truly get to know the children. You will quickly learn their personalities, their strengths and weaknesses, their likes and dislikes. It will be much easier for you to discern when someone is acting out of an impure motive or genuine desire. You will discover what works well with which children – and which children need to be reined in and which ones need to be encouraged.

2. **The leader must treat all children and what they say equally**. For example, one child might say *"The Lord showed me how the sky is blue"* and another one might say *"God took me up to the throne room and showed me a room full of gifts He wants to give to us."* The leader should respond to both revelations with the same amount of enthusiasm and affirmation. We have found it best to simply smile, nod, and warmly say something like *"That's really good"* or *"That's right."* We don't jump up and exclaim loudly every time a child

hears from God. We want to affirm and encourage them, but we don't want to make other children to feel uncomfortable or left out if God has not shown them something. The truth is, God will occasionally not speak anything just to test our motives. We tell the kids it is just as important to be truthful when God is silent as it is to speak up when He has spoken. Naturally, we encourage those who rarely share or have been reluctant in the past to share.

3. **The leader needs to be firm with the children, but not harsh.**
   Kids will be kids and will play from time to time and get too rowdy. We allow a small amount of playing as long as it is not disruptive. Some of the children will occasionally get rowdy or wild and we have to rein them back in.

   Remember, kids will be kids and God loves their curious, gentle hearts!

   We've found this is easy to do by switching gears and changing the focus - move to a different prayer station, change the tempo of the worship music, gather everyone together to sit down, or get out the praise instruments. A simple "*Michelle - we're not going to do that right now. Come over here and join the group while we ...*" can work wonders. It doesn't create a conflict between the leader and the child (where someone then has to win) and it doesn't condemn or criticize the child's behavior, it just redirects them.

   Consider making a child who is being disruptive the leader's helper, "*Travis, will you come help me get the praise instruments out so we can worship the Lord?*"

4. **Back everything you possibly can with the Word.** When a child shares something, we will often point out where the picture or idea

can be found in the Word. Sometimes it is a specific verse, at other times it is just a principle (God is a forgiving God.) When we pray for different areas, we point out why we are doing so. *"Why are we praying for Israel? Because God's Word says to 'Pray for the peace of Israel'"* or *"Let's sing and clap and dance before the Lord like it says to in Psalms."* Once again, we are training them to rely on the Word.

5. **Let the Word correct un-Biblical words, thoughts, or actions.** If a child says the Lord told him to not pay any attention to what his parents said, then we might say, *"Well, the Bible says to obey your parents and we never go against anything the Bible says."* We do not say *"That's a lie from the enemy!"* or even *"No that's not right"* or *"That's wrong."* Instead, we point out what the Bible says. Kids are smart! They can figure out where their words or actions are not the same as what we've just said. We don't need to point it out! After reminding them of what the Word says, we will usually ask if anyone else has something to share and quickly move on. Everyone makes mistakes and there is no need to dwell on it. If a child repeatedly shares un-biblical ideas or beliefs, we pull them aside and talk to them privately to find out where they are getting the information and point out specifically in the Bible what God says.

6. **Appoint a wiggly-squiggly child as your helper for at least a couple of weeks.** Keep them next to you so you can quietly direct them. Lightly touching them on the shoulder or holding their hand will be enough attention from the leader to keep them focused. In most cases, he or she will settle down after a few weeks, once they are familiar with the routine.

7. **Enforce the age limit.** We found the younger children could and would enter in for a short period of time, but often became quite

distracting by the end of the evening. Our solution was to separate the younger children into their own prayer group where they spend 15-20 minutes in praise, worship, and intercession. This time period is more appropriate for their age and attention span. After their intercession is finished, they have snack and playtime for the remainder of the evening (in a separate room). We're giving them a taste of intercession without overwhelming them and without interfering with the older children's progress.

8. **Don't go down every bunny trail.** When children bring up a subject or area that is off-topic, affirm them for hearing God, but do not automatically change the focus. *"That's really good, but let's keep praying for _____ a few more minutes."* Off-topic prayers are a very typical challenge even in adult prayer groups. Intercessors are receptors and have their spiritual antennas up. They need to learn to focus on what the group is doing and submit to the leadership and not try to insist on their own agenda – even if it is completely pure and good. During the course of an evening, we will shift gears several times and will keep in mind everything the children have brought up. Often, the child is hearing correctly and we will later pray about whatever it was they mentioned earlier. Encourage the child who initiated the topic to lead out, *"Mark, would you pray about what God showed you earlier please?"*

9. **Realize children are often very literal.** Many have a difficult time with symbolic images. For instance, once a child saw a picture of himself as a hunter shooting his bow and arrow, and then God showed him another picture of himself just sitting quietly outside in the forest. When asked what it meant, the child responded, *"I think God wants me to spend more time outside."* Thankfully, the spirit of

God quickened inside the leader the true meaning - this child was always quick to enter into spiritual warfare, which was good. God was also telling the child to spend time quietly with Him. When this meaning was shared with the child, his face brightened and he replied, "*Yeah! I've been thinking I need to make sure I'm reading my Bible every day and have a quiet time, but I haven't done it yet!*" By gently suggesting a different meaning, the child was able to receive and understand what the Lord was showing him. Notice, we did not quickly say "*That's not right!*" but instead lovingly suggested, "*Do you suppose it could mean ...*"

10. Tired children will sometimes fall asleep during our intercession. When this happens, we just let them sleep. Their spirits are still awake and participating and if their physical bodies need rest, we allow them to rest.

Using these guidelines will greatly help you maintain a good balance between correcting and crushing. Although we hold our children to a high standard of behavior, we treat them gently and with respect. We want to encourage, lead, and equip them to walk in their giftings and accomplish everything God has in store for them.

CHAPTER 7

WHEN IT ISN'T WORKING

What do you do when you spent the week seeking the Lord concerning your group, He gave you a GREAT idea, you were excited and full of anticipation as you started the time, and then it all absolutely fell flat?! It has happened to the best, so don't get discouraged. We have learned to approach the dull times with this philosophy: "There's always next week." In other words, don't obsess over it and analyze every little element and second-guess every decision and direction you made. Realize that sometimes, it's just not going to work. Do not give up! And don't underestimate the power of the Lord. To you, it may seem like nothing is happening and yet the Holy Spirit may be moving and brooding in a way we can't even comprehend or will ever know. Very rarely is prayer done in vain!

KIDS WILL BE KIDS

Remember that children are children and things in the natural can greatly affect what you are trying to do in the Spirit. For example, the kids will be more excited and a little harder to rein in on the first and last day of Christmas vacation, spring break and summer vacation. The same is true for holidays and any significant event in their lives such as a school program, play, or sports tournament. Don't try to plan a heavy, intense prayer time for those days. Concentrate on praise and worship or have a fellowship time – do something different. As they develop more of heart for prayer, the outside circumstances will become much less of a distraction.

VISITORS

Visitors are a potential distraction. We do not encourage our children to bring visitors to our intercessory group. We have not designed the group as an evangelistic outreach group – instead, visitors are always welcome at our Wednesday night and Sunday morning meetings. Despite this policy, we occasionally have visitors. When this happens, we give the visitor explanations and we try not to do anything that might offend them. Obviously, we are always obedient to the Holy Spirit, but we try to be as sensitive to the visitor as possible.

ADULTS

Carefully guard your group concerning the number of adults and the type of adults you let participate in your group. If there is a different adult in there every week, it will be disruptive. You should explain to the adults that this is a **children's** prayer group with the purpose of training the children to pray. Adults are allowed to participate but not dominate. If an adult comes on strongly, even if it is unintentional, during the beginning of the meeting, the children will become intimidated, retreat, and let the adults do the praying. Having too many adults in the meeting will have the same dampening effect. A ratio of 1 adult for every 10 children has been a good fit for us. It provides enough supervision without stifling anyone. We welcome the adult's participation in the worship, dance, and any of the prophetic acts but limit their amount of praying aloud.

RELUCTANT PARTICIPANTS

If your children are reluctant to participate in worship or prayer, we have several suggestions for you to try. First of all, **do not push or demand participation.** You want to encourage them to worship and pray without any pressure from you! Identify why your children are not participating. There are several possible reasons:

❖ **They may not know what to do**. You can correct this problem by modeling the desired behavior yourself. You as the leader should participate fully – sing, dance, worship, pray.

Provide appropriate Bible verses written in prayer format for each of your Prayer Stations. Ask individual children or groups of children to read/pray the verses aloud. *"Emily and Rebecca, will you read these verses together and the rest of us will pray silently with you."* You can also write specific prayers for the children to pray, but don't let them become a crutch – you want the children to pray from their heart and not from a piece of paper.

Make sure you are using familiar worship songs that are **easy** to sing.

❖ **Your children might not be familiar with you or each other.** Spend some time getting to know them – praise and affirm them to build up their confidence. Share your life with them so they will get to know you better. If the group does not know each other, play an "ice breaker" game at the beginning and schedule a fun activity to help build relationships.

❖ **Your children might not be comfortable with the room.** To help overcome this obstacle, make sure you are praying in a "kid-friendly" room. If they have to sit in hard adult-size chairs, it will be hard to get them engaged in prayer. They also need to have enough room to move around without having to be concerned about breaking something. At the same time, try not to use the largest room in your building because a large room tends to make them feel intimidated. The atmosphere needs to be welcoming and inviting to a child.

* **Your children might be feeling self-conscious**. During worship, turn the music up fairly loud. Encourage group activities – everyone (including you) marching around the room or dancing. Pick one of the children to lead. Praise them enthusiastically when they join in. Try to shift their focus off of themselves and onto your prayer focus.

* **Your children might not understand or have any experience in hearing God's voice**. Encourage them to share whatever they hear or see – regardless of whether it makes sense and even if it is only one word. Our children have heard single words that don't have much impact until they're put together with the other's words. Explain to them that hearing God's voice in a group is often like putting a jig-saw puzzle together – the individual pieces don't make sense until they're hooked up with the other pieces.

* **Your choice of Prayer Stations might not seem relevant to them**. Try to make the stations as personal to them as possible. Show them why you have chosen the particular stations and why they are important to your church. Include photographs and personal stories.

FOR EXAMPLE: I explain to the children why I choose the city as one of our stations. We feel as a church that God spoke to us regarding this! We are called to bless and minister to the city, not just to our own church. We are to minister to our region, not just to our own people. As the children catch this and then begin praying for their city, it develops in them a "heart" for where they live. This makes them effective in their prayers.

COMMON CHALLENGES AND QUESTIONS

Children Praying the Same thing over and over. We let the children duplicate each other's prayers as long as they are biblical. This is one of the best ways to learn to pray! If several children hear the same thing from the Lord, we point out how they are praying together in unity. We take the opportunity to explain how the Lord will often speak the same thing to multiple people to emphasize the point, or to encourage them and to train them to hear His voice. If it seems like the duplicating prayers are getting out of hand, then designate one or two children to lead and instruct the others to pray silently in agreement.

Discipline Challenges. The only time we have experienced discipline challenges has been when a parent brings a child who has no interest in praying. If the child is continually disruptive, you should kindly explain the purpose of this group is to pray and being disruptive is not fair to the other children. If they still don't want to join in and continue to be disruptive, it may not be the right time for that particular child to participate. The child may not have the spiritual maturity or understanding at this time. However, don't discourage them from ever participating in your prayer group. Suggest that the child "try again" in a few months. Children are constantly changing and maturing and he/she may very well be able to participate in a short period of time.

Need to Interpret. You do not have to be responsible for explaining and interpreting everything the children see or hear. Correct anything unbiblical – but you don't have to interpret everything. First ask the children what they think it means because they will often have at least part of the understanding. Symbols can have many different meanings and children often interpret them differently from adults. If the child does not know the meaning, then ask the Lord to reveal it, "*Lord we ask for more* *understanding on this.*" You can also use a book on dreams and symbolism to give you additional insight. We don't recommend spending time during prayer to look up symbols – have the child look it up afterwards.

EVALUATE

If it seems like you are not making any progress week after week, then you need to evaluate what you are doing. Don't keep doing the same thing over and over and expect it to eventually "click." Shake things up a little - change the order or the setting. Choose different songs or change the type of music; ask someone to play the keyboard or guitar instead of using pre-recorded music or vice versa. Read the chapter "Variety, Variety, Variety" in this manual for more ideas. Be flexible and be creative. It's easy to get stuck in a rut because ruts are usually comfortable and require less effort.

> *Don't keep doing the same thing over and over and expect it to eventually "click."*

Be willing to change whatever is not working regardless of why it was started in the beginning or how well it worked then. We started with Prayer Stations, but we seldom use them now. Children are complex - most enjoy routines, but will become bored with something after it becomes very familiar to them. Ask the Lord to give you creative ideas and strategies. He knows your kids even better than you do and He wants the group to succeed even more than you do.

SEEK THE LORD

Put your spiritual antennas up – see what the Lord is doing in other ministries, other countries. Read magazine articles, books, or use the Internet to increase your awareness of how the Holy Spirit is moving and then incorporate these materials into your group. Share with the children what you've discovered and ask the Lord together to give you new, fresh revelation. Include them in asking the Lord for a more effective prayer time. (We do not recommend telling the children *"This is not going very well."* Phrase it in the positive, *"Let's ask the Lord to speak to our hearts,"* or, *"Ask the Lord to show us more."*)

CHAPTER 8

PERSONALITIES AND GIFTINGS

In order to have an effective prayer group, you need to learn to recognize the different personalities and giftings God has placed in your children. Personalities and giftings are given to us so it is pointless and frustrating to try to fit every child into the same mold. Spend time observing your children even when they are not in your group. Watch their behavior and their reactions (Reactions often tell you more about the child than their deliberate behavior). Some children are animated and dramatic, others are quiet and factual. Some are eager to participate and share, others are more reluctant. Some want (and need) to lead, others want (and need) to follow. *All want to be understood and appreciated.*

Recognizing the different giftings and personalities in your group will help you in equipping them more effectively. Make room for all types of gifts and personalities. You will quickly notice the talkative, outspoken ones will almost always have something to share. If the Lord has not spoken to them today, they are quite happy to share what He said last night, last week, or even last year! Therefore, we are careful to ask *"What is the Lord speaking to you tonight? Not last night or last week or even this morning, I only want you to share if it was something He said tonight."* With the more eager ones, we'll verify again before letting them share. We also let them know we are always willing to listen to what they have to say privately, before or after the meeting.

Quieter children need more encouragement and time to share. We will specifically ask the quieter children by name, *"Susan, do you have anything you want to share?"* This gives them permission and time to share and it also allows them an easy way to say no. They are not saying God did not speak to them, they are only saying they don't want to share what God said. During prayer times, we will ask a quieter child if he would like to pray for a specific need, *"Caleb, would you like to pray for the President?"* If they decline, we usually pick whoever is eagerly waving their hand and shouting, *"I will, I will!"*

We will also specifically ask a child to read a portion of Scripture aloud, *"Wendy, would you please read Psalms 51 for us?"* (Be sure to pick someone who likes to read aloud.) Another tactic is to just say to the group, *"Let's let someone who hasn't prayed aloud yet have a turn."* The ones who have already gone learn to wait and let everyone have a turn. If no one speaks up, we call on a child we know will pray. This way, everyone learns prayer etiquette and how to be a team player.

Some children are born leaders and administrators. We have one child who will appear to be disengaged from the rest of the group quietly sitting to the side. At some point she comes to the leader with a somewhat elaborate plan to perform a prophetic act. We let her direct the other children and arrange everything according to the way she "saw" it. It is usually creative, on focus, and includes all of the children. Because the idea came from another child, the others are quite willing to participate. We are allowing this young leader to exercise her leadership skills under our watchful eye.

Watch with discernment and learn the giftings God has given to the kids in the group. Instill their natural gifts when they are young!

Some children are born servants and truly have a need to help, so we allow them to help setup the room or cleanup afterwards. These children are thanked and affirmed in the same manner as those who are being leaders. We work very hard to make room for and appreciate all. We also incorporate the children into all areas of our church life. Those who love to serve are encouraged to serve in the Helps Ministry as greeters and ushers along with the adults. One family even allows their children to help clean the church.

One child worked very hard to learn to play on the keyboard two songs we often sang. She was then allowed to play those songs on the keyboard for several weeks during worship. It was exciting to see the satisfaction on her face in being allowed to use her gift of music in our prayer group.

There are others who are extremely gifted in dance, so we periodically allow time for them to dance before the Lord. We have a wide assortment of flags, banners, scarves, and praise instruments available for them to use. Still others are wonderful artists - so we allow them to draw prophetic pictures on the chalkboard, whiteboard, and paper.

Some of our children are more interested in the nations that others. When we pray for specific countries, we'll ask them to share what they know about the country or the people. This is also true for current events. One family in particular is very informed politically, so we try to include them when praying for the United States, the elections, the President, and other current events.

When we pray for the sick, we call on those who have an interest in healing or a heart of compassion (you will know who these are - they always have a long list of friends, neighbors, and relatives who need prayer). We also allow our children to minister on the Healing Room teams with the adults.

We give the children who like to teach the opportunity to use their giftings. They will present a short lesson to the group – one they have prayed and studied about. The other children love listening to the child-teacher. They will completely listen to everything the child-teacher says and does, regardless of how well the lesson is taught!

Generally, we try to include everyone and provide a variety of experiences in prayer. This way, we expose them to more than just what comes naturally to them. We give them experience in using their giftings and talents individually and also in being a team player with the group. Once again, these are things we want them to do when they are adults. Therefore, we are instilling these traits in them while they are young.

CHAPTER 9

VARIETY, VARIETY, VARIETY

Although children need structure and routine, they also tend to get bored with the same thing week after week. Therefore, we intentionally plan "breaks" in our routine. We are constantly tweaking, changing and growing the format of the group. We keep the date, time, and leadership of the group consistent but we change the **format** just enough to make it exciting without making it hectic.

Several times a year, we plan fun activities. These events have a dual purpose: to prevent boredom and to develop relationships. The events don't have to be elaborate, just simply getting together and having fun with each other. We've had swimming parties, sleepovers, and picnics. These activities are special rewards for those who have worked hard and have consistently attended our prayer group.

In addition to special events, we'll change aspects of our regular prayer night such as going to a different room to pray - we've prayed in the Youth Room, the sanctuary, the Children's Church room and even outside of the building. One very powerful time occurred when we walked the perimeter of our church property and called to the North, South, East, and West to give up souls. We spent several minutes facing a low-income housing project bordering our church property. The children called aloud, welcoming the children from the apartments, saying things such as "You are welcome here! God loves you! He wants you! We want you!" At the time, there was no one outside listening. The next night, several children from the apartments attended our Wednesday evening program!

We also take occasional field trips to various places to pray. We have gone to schools, city hall, neighborhoods, and a pro-life women's clinic. We now go to the clinic once a month to pray for the counselors, the women, their babies, and to also pray for life. We always have extra adult supervision on these trips and we remind the kids numerous times what we are praying about. *"This is the time to pray for these unborn babies and their mothers. We're not going to pray for healing or for other nations. Tonight, whatever you pray needs to be related to these babies and their mothers."*

We will also mix up the order of the evening or change the setup of the room. We will introduce a new worship song and teach the actions to it. We'll switch the type of worship music - use CDs instead of live people or bring someone in on the keyboard or guitar.

We are also constantly looking and reading about what is going on in the Spirit in our nation and other parts of the world. We will share with the kids what the prophets are saying (in short segments of course). We read to them what other kids are doing in other states and countries to encourage and inspire them. We have also read to them about past revivals and how God used children during those revivals.

Purposefully schedule a few extra activities using some of our ideas, or create your own. Just do something to prevent your group from getting into a rut. You will see for yourself that variety will increase the level of interest and will help keep your group fresh.

CHAPTER 10

TAKING IT TO THE NEXT LEVEL

WHAT NEXT?

Once your prayer group is well established and they have learned the concept of prayer, you can step out of the station model and learn other areas of prayer. When we reached this point, we began introducing our children to the concept of soaking (listening) prayer. We started slowly and gradually increased the amount of time spent on soaking prayer. Once again, we were amazed at the depth of the revelation the children were receiving from these times and how willing they were to participate. Soaking prayer will lead the children into intimacy with the Lord. Then their prayers will come out of a relationship with the Lord and not just a religious activity. Soaking prayer will naturally lead your children into a deeper maturity with the Lord. Therefore, we encourage you to take similar steps with your group by introducing them to soaking prayer.

Of all the different ways you can mentor the children to hear God, I have found this to be the most fruitful!

SOAKING PRAYER: WHAT IS IT?

First of all, let's define the term "Soaking Prayer". It is a popular phrase referring to lying quietly before the Lord in prayer. It is not a time of requesting anything from the Lord or even praising and worshipping Him. Instead, it is a time of lying quietly in His presence, fellowshipping with Him silently, and meditating on Him.

Using the word "Soaking" originates from the Greek word *baptizo*, which literally means "to immerse, to submerge, to saturate." The word "Baptizo" was first used in an ancient recipe for making pickles out of cucumbers. The cucumber is first dipped ("Bapto") into boiling water and then placed ("Baptizo") into a vinegar solution for a period of time. When it was "Baptizo" it was changed from a cucumber into a pickle – the hard outer skin is made soft and pliable. The idea of soaking prayer is to saturate yourself in the presence of the Lord in such a way that you will be changed afterwards. Areas of your life that were once hard or stony places become soft and pliable to the Lord.

BENEFITS OF SOAKING PRAYER

We have found numerous benefits to leading the children in soaking prayer:

1. Teaches them the biblical concept of hearing God's still, small voice.
2. Trains them to hear God's voice.
3. Creates an intimate relationship with the Lord.
4. Tears down the expectation of always being entertained.
5. Bypasses their mind, therefore allowing children with learning disabilities to enter in and participate.
6. Envelops the reluctant or resistant child with the Lord's presence in such a way that will affect their heart over time.

HOW TO SET UP A SOAKING PRAYER TIME

We suggest you use these guidelines when your prayer group is ready to participate in a soaking prayer time:

1. You want the children to have an understanding on this type of prayer, so it's important to know yourself what the Bible says about this type of prayer, lying quietly before the Lord, meditating on Scripture and descriptions of experiencing God. Once you are familiar with these concepts, briefly teach them to your children:
   - Think and meditate on Scriptures that would draw their heart to God. Pick verses or concepts that you want to develop in their heart.
   - For example: John 3:16, as they think about that verse quietly they will start to realize how much God loves them.

> *"It will build in them a heart of worship because of what is going on in the throne room."*
>
> - REVELATION 4:1

2. Each session, briefly remind the children about soaking prayer:
   - It is not a time for prayer requests.
   - It is not a time of praise and worship.
   - It is not the time to let your mind wander or think about school, activities, friends, or anything else.
   - It is a time of focusing on the Lord.

3. Instruct the children to lie still before the Lord:
   - Allow them to get in a comfortable, relaxed position. We keep an assortment of pillows, blankets, and beanbag chairs for this purpose.

- Encourage them to quiet their thoughts and their mind.
- Softly play instrumental worship music.
- If possible, turn the lights low (not off).

You constantly have to help them keep focused; remember this is training ground. I will say, *"Think about the verse, what is God saying?"*, etc.

4. Ask the Lord to show them what He wants to show them, *"Oh Lord, will you please reveal yourself to us? Show us, Lord, whatever you want to show us."* Sometimes, we'll ask Him something specific such as, *"Show us your throne room, Lord"* or *"Lord, "put on our heart what is on Your heart.."*

5. Encourage the children to expect Him to show them something and to wait quietly until He does. We usually remind them of the following:

- They will probably not see anything with their physical eyes.
- The Lord usually speaks or shows them things through their imagination.
- Occasionally, children will actually smell, taste, hear, or feel something.
- Always be honest – do not make something up just because your friends are seeing or experiencing something.

6. Start small first – spend only 15-20 minutes on soaking prayer. As they become accustomed to it, they will be able to spend longer periods of time soaking.

7. Afterwards, ask the children to share what they saw or experienced and journal any significant or recurring pictures.

CHAPTER 11

WORKING WITH YOUR CHURCH LEADERSHIP

Since my husband and I are senior pastors and elders in our church government, I realize I have had an advantage over many of you. We did not have to go through a bunch of red tape to establish a children's prayer group. Our entire church leadership loves what God is doing in the children and are extremely supportive.

For some churches, a children's prayer group may be a new concept and will need to be submitted to the leadership for approval. You might need to present your idea to one or more church leaders and you might not be able to start the group as quickly as you would like to start. As one who is in authority in a local church, I would like to offer a few guidelines that I believe will help get your children's prayer group off to a sound, correct start.

1. GOD IS A GOD OF ORDER. God established leadership structure and it is not unspiritual to go through the right channels. In fact, quite the opposite is true: Authority is given for our benefit and protection. Follow your church's procedure for establishing new areas of ministry.

2. PLOW IN THE SPIRIT REALM FIRST. Before you request permission from your church leadership, spend a lot of time praying. Plow in the spiritual realm first by praying for favor, revelation for your church government, and clarity as you explain your idea. Wait until the Lord tells you to go forward. Walk in the fruit of the Spirit when you communicate your request to your leadership. (Love, joy, peace, patience, kindness, goodness, gentleness, faithfulness, and *self-control!*)

3. SUBMIT. If your church leadership does not feel the timing is right or they don't see that it's God, submit to their decision. Do not speak evil of them or grumble and complain to others about them. Go back to your prayer closet and get direction from the Lord. Maybe it's not the right timing yet. Never react in rebellion. You do not want to build your group on a foundation of rebellion. And you especially do not want to transfer that rebellion to the kids.

4. BUILD UP. Your children's prayer group should be like any other ministry or program in your church in that it should build up and not tear down your church. Do not let the prayer group become a source of strife or conflict. It should be a blessing to your church! **If a church member questions the validity of your group, take the opportunity to educate them. Do not get offended or react defensively.**

5. STAY WITHIN YOUR CHURCH'S DOCTRINE. While leading your children's prayer group, do not teach or allow anything to happen to contradict your church's doctrinal statement. If your church does not embrace the gifts of the Holy Spirit, do not teach your children to pray in tongues. Stay under the authority of your church by adhering to its doctrinal beliefs.

6. ENCOURAGE YOUR CHURCH LEADERSHIP TO MAKE ROOM FOR THE CHILDREN ON SUNDAY MORNINGS. As your group matures, your children will begin to participate more in the worship service on Sunday mornings. Encourage your leadership to allow them to participate and watch for opportunities to encourage your children to participate. It is best if you discuss this possibility with your church leadership first (not on a Sunday morning). Meet with them and explain what the children have been doing during the prayer group meetings. Ask them for permission to allow the children to share words of knowledge, songs, prophetic words, prayers, and verses. Instruct your children to follow the protocol of your church, and encourage them to be bold enough to submit it to the leadership.

WHEN THE ANSWER IS NO

If your church leadership declines your request to start a children's prayer group, do not give up! Continue to pray and consider other avenues in your community. See if there is another organization such as a home school group, a youth center, a daycare program, or a Bible club that would welcome this type of ministry. Perhaps you should consider gathering your neighbourhood children together. Out of respect to your church government, you should not gather a group of children from just your church. Seek the Lord and ask Him for the right mix of children and the right season.

CHAPTER 12

EQUIPPING TO PRAY FOR A LIFETIME

"IS THERE NOT A CAUSE?"

We have been amazed how the children, even at their young age, love a "Cause" or "Purpose." Once your children's prayer group is firmly established, we encourage you to take on a prayer focus outside the church. This focus will develop in your children a heart for areas outside of your church walls.

The pro-life cause has been our "out of the church walls" focus. It is a cause very much on the heart of God and it is important to develop that same heart in our children. A friend in the ministry, Lou Engle, has taken on the pro-life issue for our nation by establishing a 24/7 prayer in Washington, D.C., for the reversal of Roe vs. Wade. Lou believes God has shown him that raising up children across our nation to pray for LIFE is going to be a key for overturning this law. With that insight in mind we strongly encourage you to consider taking on this prayer focus - once your group is ready.

KEYS TO DEVELOPING HEARTS FOR PRO-LIFE

- Give the children appropriate understanding about abortion – (Establish a definition that best fits your group.)
- Use the Word to show what you believe about this topic:
    Psalms 139
    Jeremiah 1:5

- Give the children age-appropriate choices on how you pray. I always want love to be our hearts on this topic for the ones we are praying for.
- You might also consider using the Sanctity of Human Life curriculum developed by The Center for Moral Clarity.

We chose to activate our group with the pro-life cause by going once a month to a local pro-life clinic. This particular clinic in our city encourages girls and women who are contemplating abortion to choose life. They also provide resources and assistance for those who choose not to abort their babies. We take our prayer group and walk through the area, praying for all aspects of the clinic. (Safety, protection, effectiveness, and for the Light of God to shine.) The children take this opportunity very seriously and love to pray for others.

CHOOSE A CAUSE

There are many outreach areas you could choose as a cause for your group. Once again, pray and ask the Lord for direction. Possible areas or "causes" could be:

> *Children take this opportunity very seriously and love to pray for others!*

- ❖ Hospitals (Praying for the sick)
- ❖ Nursing Home
- ❖ Homeless shelters
- ❖ Cities (walking the streets and praying for the city you live in)
- ❖ Government (walk around government buildings)
- ❖ Schools (walk around the school or playground area)

Please use wisdom when selecting a time and place to take the children to pray. We always take extra adults to supervise and we pray at a time when the clinic is not open.

Developing a heart in the children for causes outside of their own church walls will produce several results:

- ❖ Give them a BIGGER picture that just themselves
- ❖ Will develop a heart of evangelism in them
- ❖ Equips them in many different focuses of prayer
- ❖ Plus, it will totally bless the area they are praying for

The Lord is raising up a generation who know their God and will do great exploits for Him!

FINAL WORD

Our prayer for you as you begin to equip the next generation in the area of prayer is that you would capture God's heart toward His children. We pray you would have the privilege of leading children into many encounters with Him. We hope you will use this manual as a tool to help you build, build, build, a structure that will house a children's prayer movement in your area. We have the responsibility to mentor what some are calling the "Josiah Generation": A generation of boys and girls who will turn to the Lord with all their heart, with all their soul, and with all their might; children with tender hearts who seek after HIS PRESENCE. They don't want to serve God through religious traditions but instead, want to encounter Him in a real and tangible way.

God bless you as together we build a platform for the next generation to GO further than we did in the things of God.

Carol Koch
Children on the Frontline
cofl@xpministries.com

MINISTRY BIOGRAPHY

Pastor Carol Koch

Carol Koch and husband Alan have served as senior pastors of Christ Triumphant Church in Lee's Summit, Missouri, since the church was established in 1984. Carol ministers weekly to both children and adults. She is an encourager, equipper, intercessor, and carries an apostolic mantle. She turned a faltering mid-week children's program into a dynamic, Holy Spirit-led ministry. In 2002, Carol started the children's prayer group, which led to the creation of this manual. Carol's passion is to see that all believers, regardless of age, gender, or race become effectively equipped to do the work of the ministry.

CPSIA information can be obtained
at www.ICGtesting.com
Printed in the USA
FSOW04n1925040617
34728FS